Gotcha Day

A Carried In My Heart
Adoption Story for Children

Gotcha Day

A Carried In My Heart
Adoption Story for Children

Written by
Rebecca Tabasso

Illustrated by
Bonnie Lemaire

www.carriedinmyheart.com

For Sean and Danny-Always.
You have brought me so much joy.
I love you and am so blessed to have *Gotcha!*

Carried In My Heart Books is a division of Carried In My Heart, LLC, 55 Hidden Valley Drive, Newark, DE 19711

ISBN: 0615631320
ISBN-13: 9780615631325
Library of Congress Control Number: 2012906914
Carried In My Heart Books, Newark, DE

A Word from the Author

Every adoption is uniquely special, and each family celebrates in their own very personal way. One constant, however, is the love for their child as they celebrate. Our family chose the tradition of celebrating "Gotcha Day". We see the use of the term Gotcha as in a warm, safe embrace—akin to the deeply loving sentiment spoken when consoling a hurt or scared child, holding them in your arms and softly saying, "I've got you." I, as an adult adoptee, and our children who came to us through adoption, love this tradition. It is one of many ways we celebrate the creation of our family, our many blessings, and each other. We've also used "Gotcha Day" as one of many ways to initiate and maintain an open dialogue about adoption with our children.

I hope you find *Gotcha Day: A Carried In My Heart Adoption Story for Children* engaging and fun as you share it with your child and a warm, special way to personalize and share your own family's adoption story as you journey through the book. It is packed with opportunities to discuss the holidays and traditions that fit your family, the characteristics and traits that make your child uniquely special, as well as your family's own unique "Gotcha Day" story.

— Rebecca Tabasso

Suzie was enjoying spaghetti and mega meatballs with her family when her mother announced, "A special day is coming, Suzie. Do you know which special day it is?"

Suzie loved guessing games. "Is it Valentine's Day? I'll make Valentines," she said with excitement in her voice. "Will you be mine?"

"I will always be yours, but no, it is not Valentine's Day."

"Is it St. Patrick's Day? I could wear my lucky green shirt," said Suzie.

"No, my wee lass, 'tis not St. Patrick's Day either. Guess again."

"Or is it Halloween?" Suzie grinned. "I love Halloween! Costumes, parties, and trick-or-treating. Hmm, maybe I'll dress up as a scary monster or maybe even a funny clown."

Suzie's mother smiled. "No, try again. The special day is not Halloween."

"Is it New Year's Eve? The party hats and noisemakers are so much fun!" Before Suzie's mother could answer, Suzie begged, "Can I stay up until midnight PLEEEAASE????"

Laughing at her excitement, Suzie's mother said, "No, honey, it isn't New Year's Eve either."

Suzie's mother thought about the special day for a moment and said, "I'll give you a clue. We'll have a big celebration and a special person will attend."

"Oh, it must be Christmas. Santa is special, and he always comes at Christmas. We better start making cookies—I think he likes chocolate chip the best." Suzie jumped up and down with excitement.

Her mother shook her head. "No, it's not Christmas."

"Then it must be Easter!" Suzie guessed. "The Easter Bunny always comes at Easter and hides beautiful colored eggs and lots of candy for us to find."

"Those are great guesses," Suzie's mother said, "but it isn't Easter either."

Suzie's mother offered another clue. "This special day is very important in our history."

Suzie groaned. Unsure of herself she asked, "Could the special day be Columbus Day, Memorial Day?" Even less certainly she added, "Or Veteran's Day?"

Suzie's mother was proud of her daughter's thoughtful guesses. She said, "Those are important days to celebrate in our country's history, but this special day isn't one of those."

"Or is it one of the special days for presidents and kings?" Suzie asked seriously, but growing more and more uncertain.

Hiding a smile, Suzie's mother copied her serious tone. "Those are very important days in our history, too, but no, the special day coming isn't President's Day or Martin Luther King, Jr. Day."

"I'll give you one last clue," her mother said. "There might even be balloons, or cake, or presents."

"My birthday! I can't believe I didn't think of that first." Suzie bubbled with relief and excitement.

"You're getting closer, but it isn't your birthday either," her mother encouraged. "Try again."

Suzie reviewed all her previous guesses,
ticking them off on her fingers. Valentine's,
St. Patrick's, Halloween. Not New Year's,
Christmas, or Easter. It wasn't Columbus,
Memorial, or Veteran's Day or those days
for presidents or kings, either. AND, it
wasn't her birthday.

What WAS the special day she
was forgetting???

☑ A Big CELEBRATion

☑ ONe Special PERSon

☑ Family HiStoRY

"Let's look at all of the clues together," her mother said. "It is a special day; it's one we celebrate; it may even be celebrated with balloons, cake, or presents; there is a special person attending; AND it is an important day in our history—our family history."

Suddenly Suzie's face lit up and she laughed. "I've got it! I've got it!"

Suzie's mother said, "Well then, tell me what you've got."

"The special day is my...GOTCHA DAY!" Suzie yelled.

"That's right, Suzie!" Her mother smiled and hugged her tight. "YOU are the special person we celebrate each anniversary of the day we became a family. We had been wishing for someone just like you to make our family complete. You are so kind and loving, a beautiful young girl. You are so smart, and your love of games, your excitement, and your happy nature brighten our family and make you all the more special."

Suzie hugged her mom back and said, "Tell me about my Gotcha Day again."

"The day we became a family is a very important day in our family's history. I will always remember the first time I held you in my arms. You were so tiny, yet you grabbed ahold of my hair tightly, as if you were never going to let go. It was as if you were saying, 'You're mine.' When we brought you home, we held your first Gotcha Day celebration with all of our family and friends who came to welcome you and celebrate your adoption. We will always remember and celebrate the day we gotcha and how much we love you."

"And the day I got you too," Suzie added with a smile.

Several days later, Suzie ran into the family room
and found it decorated with all her favorite colors.
There were pink and purple balloons, pink and purple
streamers, and even a frosted pink cake with a
purple border. Her eyes grew wider as she saw the
table filled with some of her favorite foods, including

her mom's homemade ham and pineapple pizza.
   She felt really special. Best of all, Suzie felt
very loved when she saw her whole family.
   They held out their arms and shouted,
"HAPPY GOTCHA DAY!"

Gotcha Day Certification

$\mathcal{T}$his is to Certify that the Official Gotcha Day
For the below-named, Very Loved, and Special Person

_____

(Name)

is

_____

(Date)

$\mathcal{L}$et it hereby be known by this special person that your
Gotcha Day is a very important date in our family history and
how happy we are to have Gotcha!

_____   _____

Signature   Signature

www.carriedinmyheart.com

14726643R00018

Made in the USA
Charleston, SC
27 September 2012